Career Exploration

Careers If You Like Working with Your Hands

Toney Allman

ReferencePoint Press®

San Diego, CA

© 2020 ReferencePoint Press, Inc.
Printed in the United States

For more information, contact:
ReferencePoint Press, Inc.
PO Box 27779
San Diego, CA 92198
www.ReferencePointPress.com

LIBRARY OF CONGRESS CATALOGING-IN-PUBLICATION DATA

Names: Allman, Toney, author.
Title: Careers If You Like Working with Your Hands/by Toney Allman.
Description: San Diego, CA: ReferencePoint Press, Inc., [2019] | Series:
  Career Exploration series | Includes bibliographical references and index.
  | Audience: Grade 9 to 12.
Identifiers: LCCN 2018060429 (print) | LCCN 2019013665 (ebook) | ISBN
  9781682826003 (eBook) | ISBN 9781682825990 (hardback)
Subjects: LCSH: Building trades—Vocational guidance—Juvenile literature. |
  Fire extinction—Vocational guidance—Juvenile literature. | Makeup
  artists—Vocational guidance—Juvenile literature. | Mechanical
  engineering—Vocational guidance—Juvenile literature. |
  Agriculture—Vocational guidance—Juvenile literature. |
  Medicine—Vocational guidance—Juvenile literature. | Vocational
  guidance—Juvenile literature.
Classification: LCC TH159 (ebook) | LCC TH159 .A54 2019 (print) | DDC
  331.702—dc23
LC record available at https://lccn.loc.gov/2018060429

Contents

Hands On

According to the University of Kent in the United Kingdom, the first step in choosing a career is self-awareness. This means understanding yourself and knowing your interests, skills, personality, and values. Interests include such factors as what a person enjoys doing, the kinds of activities one chooses to engage in, and the ways a person may prefer to work. Values may include things like a wish to help others, a desire to contribute to society in a meaningful way, a need to be independent, or a motivation to be challenged and take risks. Interests and values are part of the personality, but other aspects of personality may affect career choices too. These may involve characteristics such as assertiveness, being outgoing or reserved, and persistence in the face of obstacles. Skills are not specific educational skills but rather the abilities and talents you have had since you were born or that you developed throughout your life. Examples of such skills are athletic ability, being good with language and words, or manual dexterity. Understanding your interests, values, skills, and personality is very helpful for recognizing the kind of career you may enjoy the most.

Of course, people have multiple skills, interests, and values, so it is important to choose a career that matches not only your personality but also your abilities. The University of Kent offers the example of a gifted athlete who has a strong interest in athletics and the personality and values necessary for a successful athletic career. Not everyone interested in sports and athletics, however, has the skills to play professionally. Still, that interest can determine career choices. As the University of Kent explains, "Some may enter sports-related careers, in leisure management, sports administration or promotion, retailing sporting goods or teaching PE [physical education]. Others will seek out careers in different fields that offer similar opportunities for physical activity, teamwork, competition or challenge."[1] It all depends on the individual. What matters is determining what activities you most enjoy and how your interests and abilities could lead to a career. Some people like athletics, some like music, some enjoy writing, and some like making things with their hands.

Realistic Types of People

During the 1970s, psychologist John L. Holland described six basic personality types that correspond to six work environments. He developed assessment tools to determine individual interests and compatible work environments. The six types and environments are *realistic*, *investigative*, *artistic*, *social*, *enterprising*, and *conventional*. People can be combinations of these different types, but most are strongest in one area, with one or two other areas of interest. Today, the Holland codes are often used to help people choose a career and to determine what kinds of jobs might be suitable for them.

People who like to work with their hands are realistic types. They are problem solvers who are practical and independent. They prefer to deal with concrete information and to be able to see and measure the results of their work. They are often skilled at assembling, repairing, and working with machines, animals, plants, or tools. They are hands-on people who enjoy accomplishing things and exploring the world with their hands and eyes. They deal very well with the physical world.

Finding the Perfect Match

Realistic people may also be artistic and enjoy creating things. A chef, for example, has a passion for cooking and creating meals. The Holland code interest areas for chefs include building (realistic), creating (artistic), and persuading (enterprising). Executive chef Thomas Zacharias loves food and cooking. He says, "Of all the traits one needs to . . . be truly happy in this line of work, being passionate is perhaps the most vital. Passion for food, serving people, the energy of a busy kitchen and leading a team of motivated cooks has its own challenges, and rewards."[2]

Other realistic people may love working with animals. Dog groomers, for example, have practical, hands-on skills that are combined with a love of animals, an artistic interest in making a dog look beautiful, and an ability to handle the challenges of a difficult grooming or an animal that may be frightened or resistant. Others who like animals may prefer to work outdoors and perhaps run a horseshoeing business or provide veterinary care to livestock.

For some realistic people, the construction business offers the ultimate satisfaction in working with their hands. The project management company Fieldlens writes, "How many professionals in other industries can point at the brand-new hospital in town and say, 'I helped build that'? Whether it's a road, a home, a sewage system or a school, the things you build matter."[3]

If you are realistic, practical, like seeing the results of your work, and want real-world problems to solve, then a hands-on career may be for you. Thousands of different jobs are waiting.

Electrician

A Few Facts

Number of Jobs
666,900

Median Pay
$54,110 in 2017

Educational Requirements
High school diploma or equivalent

Personal Qualities
Critical-thinking and problem-solving skills; attention to detail; physical stamina and strength; good color vision

Work Settings
Indoors and outdoors for almost every kind of building

Future Job Outlook
9 percent job growth through 2026

What Does an Electrician Do?

Electricians install, maintain, and repair electrical power, communications, and control systems in almost every kind of building, including homes, businesses, and industrial settings. They may work on wiring and electrical components, such as circuit breakers, transformers, and outlets, and they know how to use hand tools, power tools, and electrical testing devices. They read blueprints and diagrams. They need to be familiar with state and federal safety regulations for electrical components. Electricians may install complete electrical systems in newly constructed buildings or maintain electrical systems in existing buildings. Whatever they do, they must have a thorough grasp of how electricity works and how to safely handle electrical problems.

Commonly, a service or residential electrician is called upon to fix an electrical problem. Perhaps the lights in a home are flickering, or an outlet is not working, or a small business has no power at all. Before attempting to diagnose the issue and find the source of the failure, the electrician must ensure that no electricity is running through

A Hero in the Central Intelligence Agency

"I found myself overseas heading out to a compound to try to fix an electrical safety issue. . . . I showed up, tool bag in hand, and when I arrived I was surrounded by good, hard working people that had tons of electrical issues they were hoping I could help them with. I was able to fix the original issue pretty quickly and . . . I started working on the other problems they had. I fixed lighting circuits, camera systems, grounding issues, you name it. If it was an electrical issue, this place had it, and I was the only electrician for hundreds of miles."

—An electrician with the US Central Intelligence Agency

Quoted in Central Intelligence Agency, "A Day in the Life of a Field Utility Systems Specialist," August 6, 2018. www.cia.gov.

the wiring or equipment that must be tested. Typically, he or she tests for electrical current using an instrument called a volt stick. Once certain the power is off, the electrician can begin to search for the source of the electrical failure. Electrician Nate Nord explains, "You're trying to figure something out at least 50% of the time. That's a normal day in the life of an electrician – troubleshooting."[4]

Using logic and experience, Nord usually finds the problem area. He may discover that a circuit breaker has overloaded or shorted out and must be replaced. Once he does that, he can turn the power back on and check that everything is working correctly and safely before he leaves for his next call. Nord says that service electricians may visit six homes a day, solving different electrical issues. Diagnosis and repair can take time, however. Good electricians have to be patient and meticulous no matter how many service calls lie ahead. Electricians do not allow a busy schedule to hurry them into making a mistake or doing a job incorrectly.

A commercial or industrial electrician's job may be more extensive than a residential one. An electrician can trace the flow of electrical energy to and from circuit breakers and transformers and replace faulty or outdated wiring when needed or install new wiring and electrical equipment, such as light fixtures, water heaters, or solar panels. He or she may maintain and install generators and electrical machines inside factories. Whatever the job, electricians have to be prepared to think on their feet. As electrician Matt Day explains,

> Typically for commercial and industrial jobs, although not always, an architect or engineer will create a layout of where the electrical equipment (i.e. conduit, receptacles, lights, junction boxes, distribution panels, wiring, etc.) will be installed. Once the inside wiremen arrive on the job they begin installing said equipment. Inevitably we will have to make some alterations or additions to the original plans, because in the real world, things change.[5]

A Typical Workday

An electrical contractor working in commercial construction might spend days or weeks working on the same project, but a residential electrician's days are very different. Michael Lucas, for example, is a residential electrician with Berwick Electric Company in Colorado Springs, Colorado. He begins the day at the shop each morning with a cup of coffee shared with the other electricians, finishing up any paperwork leftover from the previous day, and getting a list of the day's appointments. Then he gets into his service van to drive to the various jobs. The scheduled appointments are always interesting to him because each is so different. At one call, he may have the challenging job of identifying a "loose neutral"—which is no easy task. "Solving electrical problems can be like playing detective," he says.

> A loose neutral is literally a neutral wire that has gone loose somewhere in the house and is wreaking havoc with the voltage in the rest of the house. These aren't easy to find, as they can be located in the switchbox, an outlet, a light fixture, in the attic, in the panel, at the meter, or even out

[in the wiring coming into the house from the street]. As an electrician you really have to think logically in order to figure it out.[6]

Sometimes, the jobs are unexpectedly fast and easy. At one home, Lucas was asked to remove a broken kitchen garbage disposal and replace it with a new one. Just as he was getting started, Lucas discovered there was actually nothing wrong with old disposal. The homeowners had simply not pushed the re-set button. He explains, "Many people aren't aware that most garbage disposals have reset buttons on the bottom. When a garbage disposal is too full, the motor has trouble moving and it overheats (called thermal overload). Usually all you have to do is push a reset button!"[7] Such jobs may not demand much exper-tise, but others are complex.

Lucas and a team of other electricians spent hours and a lot of creative thought solving a loss of power for a large communi-cations company. A transformer had blown when high voltage coursed through it, causing the two other transformers for the building to fail also. The team had to figure out a safe way to get a temporary power supply to the building until they could complete the lengthy, complex job of repairing the damaged transformers.

Education and Training

With a high school diploma, most would-be electricians go through an apprenticeship program, but others start by attend-ing a technical training or vocational school. These schools teach basic electrical information, circuitry, and safety, and they typically require one or two years to complete. Generally, such training counts as one thousand to two thousand hours of work expe-rience toward an electrician's license. On-the-job experience of four to five years (eight thousand to ten thousand hours) is usually required for an apprentice electrician to be licensed and certi-fied as a journeyman electrician and work alone. Apprenticeship programs are available through unions in every state through the

An electrician checks a circuit breaker box to determine whether it is the source of a problem. Electricians install and maintain commercial and residential electrical systems and troubleshoot electrical problems when they arise.

International Brotherhood of Electrical Workers and the National Electrical Contractors Association. For those who do not wish to join a union, organizations such as the Independent Electrical Contractors (IEC) and the Associated Builders and Contractors offer apprenticeship and placement programs. An apprentice electrician works under the supervision of a licensed electrician at all times and is paid throughout the apprenticeship.

At the end of the apprenticeship program, apprentice electricians are required to take and pass their local journeyman electrician examination. With proof of apprenticeship hours and a passing score on the examination, an electrician is licensed and certified as a journeyman.

Many electricians are satisfied to remain journeymen, but some go on to earn the master electrician certification. Local jurisdictions set different qualifications for a master's license, such as four to eight years of work experience as a journeyman and passing a further examination. Master electricians are able to hire a team of electricians to work for them, become independent electrical contractors, and work for government agencies and projects.

Skills and Personality

Electricians need excellent critical-thinking and problem-solving skills, good attention to detail, and at least some mathematical and analytic ability. They must have manual dexterity and good hand-eye coordination. Electricians use a variety of tools. Common ones include pliers, wire strippers, power drills, and screwdrivers. Specialized measuring tools include ammeters (to measure electrical current), ohmmeters (to measure electrical resistance), voltmeters (to measure voltage), and oscilloscopes (to measure how voltage rises and falls). Using and understanding these tools requires both manual and intellectual ability.

In addition, electricians need to have good color vision since wiring is color coded. Color blindness could lead to wiring mistakes and property damage or even electrocution and death. Electricians generally need to be in good physical health too. They need physical strength and stamina, a good sense of balance in case they need to climb up to high places, and the ability to stand on their feet for hours at a time. They need the patience and persistence to deal with difficult problems and electrical dangers. And ultimately, they need to enjoy the idea of working with electricity and trust themselves to handle it competently.

Electricians also need to like working with people and being part of a team. As apprentices, they learn their skills from others, on the job, and journeymen continue to learn from other electricians throughout their careers. This means having good communication skills, not only with other electricians but also with other tradespeople, such as construction and building contractors. Even electricians who work alone need to be good with people since they deal with clients or employers much of the time.

Working Conditions

Electricians work both indoors and outdoors in all kinds of weather and under all kinds of conditions. Sometimes they are working in small, cramped spaces, and other times they are working at considerable heights. They are more likely to suffer injuries and accidents than tradespeople in other professions just because of the nature of their work. Such injuries include electric shocks, falls, and burns. Nevertheless, when it comes to working with electricity, these professionals are only half as likely to experience shocks and electrocutions as the general public even though electricians take ten times the risks. This is because electricians are both knowledgeable and safety conscious.

Employers and Pay

Electricians may be self-employed, work for an electrical contractor or a building contractor, or be employed by a private electrical firm. Electrician apprentices earn an average of $30,000 per year, with pay rising with experience. For a journeyman electrician, the median salary per year is $54,110. Master electricians may average between $60,000 and $70,000 per year.

What Is the Future Job Outlook for Electricians?

Job growth for electricians is expected to be about 9 percent through 2026. As the IEC explains, "Because society's need for electricity continues to be on the increase, opportunities will exist into the future regardless of changing technologies."[8]

Find Out More

Electrician Careers Guide
website: www.electriciancareersguide.com

This website offers detailed information about a career as an electrician and includes step-by-step explanations of how to become an electrician. It provides a table of contents on its home page that explains how to get started, discusses what schools and apprenticeships are available, and even includes a section for women interested in the trade.

ElectricianSchoolEdu.org
website: www.electricianschooledu.org

This comprehensive online resource offers those interested in the electrical trade information about career preparation and career progression. It has descriptions of electrician careers, lists of schools, explanations of licensing exams, and state-by-state guides on salaries, codes, and certifications.

Independent Electrical Contractors (IEC)
4401 Ford Ave., Suite 1100
Alexandria, VA 22302
website: www.ieci.org

The IEC has state chapters that offer training programs and apprenticeships as well as information for individuals interested in an electrical career. Follow the "Training" link to learn about what is available in your area.

National Electrical Contractors Association (NECA)
3 Bethesda Metro Ctr., Suite 1100
Bethesda, MD 20814
website: www.necanet.org

On the NECA website, follow the links to "Education" and "Career Information" to learn about apprenticeships and educational opportunities and for information on a career as a union electrical contractor.

Plumber

A Few Facts

Number of Jobs
480,600

Median Pay
$52,590 in 2017

Educational Requirements
High school diploma or equivalent

Personal Qualities
Mechanically inclined; critical-thinking and problem-solving ability; manual dexterity and coordination; physical strength; good communication skills

Work Settings
Indoors and outdoors in homes, businesses, factories, and any building with pipes, water supplies, or septic systems

Future Job Outlook
16 percent growth through 2026

What Does a Plumber Do?

Plumbers install and repair pipes that supply water and gas and carry away waste. They also install and maintain plumbing fixtures, such as sinks and faucets, tubs, toilets, dishwashers, washing machines, and water heaters. Some plumbers maintain septic systems and wells. Master plumbers on major construction jobs often help determine the placement of pipes and fixtures. In residences, plumbing is a critical system that must be repaired quickly when things go wrong. Without plumbers, people would not have clean running water, hot water, flush toilets, or showers. Even air conditioners, swimming pools, and gas stoves rely on plumbing fixtures. According to Mary Kennedy Thompson, the president of Mr. Rooter Plumbing, "Plumbers do a really hard job people don't want to do. . . . When we go to someone's home they are not having a good day, and our job is to turn it around for them."[9]

A Typical Workday

A plumber working in construction may expect regular working hours, but for a plumber doing residential and business service and repair, there is no such thing as a nine-to-five job. Emergencies can happen any time, whether after hours or on weekends and holidays. Typically, such a plumber is always on call. Some work for plumbing companies as a member of a team of plumbers, and some work for themselves—either alone or with a helper. Either way, plumbers never know what the next call will bring on any given day.

For many plumbers, the day starts early. Plumber Joseph Rosenblum, for example, begins his day around 5:30 a.m. so that he can go to the gym before hitting the road for his first service call. Perhaps he will be unclogging a drain at a restaurant or crawling under someone's house to find a broken pipe. Then it's on to the next job. According to Fred Schilling, a master plumber who owns his own business, plumbers spend a great deal of time each day driving from one call to the next and coping with traffic. Their trucks and vans are loaded with the tools of their trade and the spare parts that might be needed when they arrive at a job.

That next job might be unclogging a toilet. Stopped-up toilets are some of the most common problems plumbers face. And what they find causing the clog can be bizarre and funny. One plumber found a large toy dinosaur in a toilet drain. Others have found diamond rings, class rings, and dentures. At other times, plumbers may discover that the problem is not in the toilet itself but in the drain line, buried in the yard. Clearing a drain line may take hours, and plumbers may have to remove thick masses of tree roots or unidentifiable long snakes of debris.

The next call may involve replacing an old toilet with a brand new one, figuring out why outside faucets are leaking, or repairing a line to a washing machine that is leaking water all over the floor. In rural areas, the problem may be in the homeowner's well, leaving the home with no water at all. In that case, the plumber may have to repair or replace well parts and then prime the well pump by removing the air and refilling the pump with water to restart it. Whatever the trouble, a plumber is not done until the problem is solved. Rosenblum says, "You can't just drop your pipe wrench

A Skilled Profession

"The typical impression the public has of a plumber is a rough looking fellow, bent over a clogged toilet with a plunger. Nothing could be further from reality! For example, the oxygen you receive in an operating room . . . was installed by a plumber. The dental chair you sit in was installed by a plumber. The decorative fountains you enjoy while strolling Lincoln Road on Miami Beach were installed by a plumber. The gas ovens and stoves that prepare your dinner at your favorite restaurant were installed by a plumber. The pneumatic (air lines) at factories and similar facilities were installed by a plumber."

—Fred Schilling, a master plumber and business owner

Quoted in Andy Orin, "Career Spotlight: What I Do as a Plumber," *Lifehacker* (blog), February 24, 2016. https://lifehacker.com.

and say 'O.K., it's 5 o'clock, I'm going home,' and they still don't have water to their house."[10]

Each service call is different, and often a plumber does not know whether a simple complaint (such as a leaking faucet) will mean an easy fix or a complex problem. It may be an inexpensive issue or one that demands costly repairs. Steve Egner owns his own plumbing business in Washington State. He explains that a plumber has to be a diagnostician and then also clearly explain to the client what is wrong and how it must be repaired. Sometimes, just diagnosing the problem and discussing it with the homeowner can require hours of time. Egner says, "It takes a lot of discipline to give your third customer or fourth customer of the day the same level of service you gave the first customer of the day, because you're more tired. You've put 10 hours in, and you have another call to go to, and you still have to show that person the same attention and care. So, that can be really difficult."[11]

Despite the long hours many plumbers put in, they enjoy their jobs. Egner explains, "This is a great job for someone who likes variety. There are a lot of people who thrive on monotony,

Down and Dirty

"By far the worst thing about being a residential service plumber is the potential for contact with human waste. Clogged or broken sewer lines still require hands-on attention. . . . When any part of that system fails, a plumber is asked to address the most foul concentration of waste possible, and make it right again. Experience gradually hardens us to these conditions, but care must always be exercised to limit contact and prevent disease with body suits, eye protection, rubber gloves, and more."

—Plumber Steve Egner, the owner of Steve's Plumbing

Quoted in Jeremy Anderberg, "So You Want My Trade: Plumber," *Art of Manliness* (blog), October 18, 2018. www.artofmanliness.com.

and want to go to the same place every day, and do the same thing every day. That kind of job would drive me nuts."[12] Plumber Dzejn Stamenov works for Mr. Rooter Plumbing in Texas. She says, "I love plumbing! I love being able to interact with different people every day, not only serving their needs but also being able to educate them about their plumbing as well."[13]

Education and Training

Plumbers learn by doing. Most plumbers enter an apprenticeship program offered either through a union or a private plumbing contracting company. To be accepted into the program, an applicant needs to be at least eighteen years old and have a high school diploma or the equivalent. A basic math test and a drug test may also be necessary. Apprentices receive both classroom and on-the-job training. Classroom education typically involves learning about reading blueprints, safety (especially with tools and the electricity that is a component of many appliances and fixtures), and understanding local codes and regulations. On-the-job training involves working under a licensed journeyman plumber, helping to repair pipes and fixtures, perhaps soldering and welding, using tools such as pipe cutters and threading machines, and generally acting as a helper during plumbing jobs.

Apprentices are paid while they learn and generally need four to five years of job experience before they can apply to be journeyman plumbers. To be licensed as a journeyman plumber, apprentices need to demonstrate the required training and experience in each state and pass a certification examination. Those who wish to become master plumbers must go through additional training, meet further experience requirements, and pass required certification exams. They may become specialty plumbers in areas such as well drilling or industrial rigging.

Skills and Personality

Plumbing work can be physically arduous, so plumbers need the physical ability to crawl into cramped places and work while lying down. They also must have the strength to lift heavy pipes and well covers, and they need dexterity to use tools like welding torches and pipe wrenches. They work both indoors and outdoors, in all kinds of weather, and must not mind getting wet and dirty.

At the same time, plumbers are good at both listening to and communicating with people. Listening to a client's problem is the first step in troubleshooting and diagnosing a plumbing issue. And plumbers need to enjoy being investigators and have critical-thinking and problem-solving skills.

Plumbers often work alone, so they must be able to make decisions independently and be thorough, dependable, and self-motivated. They need to be persistent when a job turns out to be hard to diagnose or repair and to have patience enough to pay attention to detail. This also means being safety conscious and carefully focused on each job.

Working Conditions

Plumbing careers have a higher-than-average risk of injuries and accidents, such as burns, cuts, and falls. Plumbers may work in high places where falls are possible or find themselves in confined spaces, such as sewers, pipes, and pits, where oxygen levels are low or toxic gases are present. They may be exposed to bacteria, viruses, and parasites that could cause serious infections, and they may work around asbestos in older houses or mold growing behind sinks or tubs and in walls. Hand tools may slip, causing broken bones and deep cuts, and when power tools are used near water (which plumbers often have to do), plumbers risk burns and electrocution.

Plumbers are exposed to hazards almost daily, and in order to protect themselves, they make use of protective clothing, gloves, rubber boots, safety glasses, and disinfectants for clothing and their skin. Their working conditions are unpredictable and often stressful. Plumbing is a profession that demands a lot of dedication and a willingness to cope with extreme conditions.

Employers and Pay

Most plumbers work for private plumbing businesses, but about 10 percent are in business for themselves. Some are employed by the government or by general contractors. Median yearly pay is $52,590, and master plumbers earn on average almost $60,000 per year.

What Is the Future Outlook for Plumbers?

There is always a need for plumbers, and there is a serious shortage of plumbers in the United States. According to the US Bureau of Labor Statistics, the demand for plumbers is expected to rise 16 percent through 2026, which is much faster than average.

Find Out More

ePlumbingCourses
website: www.eplumbingcourses.com

This extensive website describes in detail what plumbers do, how to become a plumber, and what the career is like. Visitors can follow the menu links to learn about schools, apprenticeships, salaries, licensing, and more.

Plumbers Without Borders

PO Box 16082
Seattle, WA 98116
website: www.plumberswithoutborders.org

Learn about the crucial good that plumbers can do around the world as they try to prevent suffering and disease caused by the lack of access to clean water and sanitation. This volunteer organization recruits plumbers and other tradespeople to participate in community projects, such as constructing bore holes (wells) and safe latrine pits in developing countries and assisting hurricane-stricken areas in the United States to rebuild their water supply systems.

ThePlumber.com

website: https://theplumber.com

This informative website offers a multitude of articles covering the latest plumbing news, scholarship news, and much more. Its menu is categorized by general articles, history, water conservation, health and safety issues, and other educational topics concerning the world of plumbing.

United Association (UA)

Union of Plumbers, Fitters, Welders, & Service Techs
3 Park Pl.
Annapolis, MD 21401
website: www.ua.org

Representing more than 340,000 tradespeople in North America, the UA offers training and apprenticeship programs to would-be plumbers and others throughout the United States and Canada. Go to the "Training & Recruitment" link on the UA website's home page to learn what is available in your area.

HVAC Mechanic

What Does an HVAC Mechanic Do?

HVAC stands for "heating, ventilation, and air-conditioning," but some HVAC mechanics also deal with refrigeration. HVAC mechanics may also be called *technicians*. Whatever their designation, HVAC mechanics generally work on heating, ventilation, air-conditioning, and refrigeration systems that control temperature and air quality in all sorts of buildings. They install, maintain, repair, and clean these systems. Without HVAC mechanics, people would not have the comfort and health afforded by controlled temperature, humidity, and air quality in their homes and other buildings. Refrigeration systems allow for the storage and transport of foods and medicine, and HVAC mechanics ensure that these systems work as expected.

Some HVAC mechanics specialize in a certain area, such as the installation of complete systems or the maintenance and repair of systems. Others may specialize in heating, air-conditioning, solar technology, or commercial refrigeration systems. HVAC mechanics understand and work with plumbing and electrical systems too; some HVAC systems are water based, and electrical components and circuitry are an integral part of all HVAC systems.

HVAC mechanics have multiple skills and abilities. They may replace and repair defective equipment and find and repair leaks in pipes and tubing. They are able to assemble and install HVAC equipment (such as heat pumps, air-conditioning systems, and furnaces). Their tasks may also include routine replacement of filters, cleaning ducts, or refilling refrigerants.

A Typical Workday

Some days—and some jobs—are more predictable than others. Commercial HVAC mechanics who are working on major construction projects tend to have regular hours and predictable schedules. HVAC mechanics who work for themselves or for residential service and repair businesses often work on jobs that change from one day to the next. HVAC mechanic Dan Robbins explains that "HVAC is a great career for those who don't like to be in the same place day after day. Nearly every day brings a new place to work and a new issue to deal with. There is little monotony in HVAC."[14]

Bob, a retired HVAC tech from Washington State, runs the website HVAC Training 101. On his website's informational blog, he describes what may be a typical day for an HVAC mechanic who performs a variety of tasks. Perhaps the first job of the day would be a complete installation of a new heating and cooling system at a recently constructed home. There, says Bob, "the technician would move their materials into place and start working on connecting things like pumps, fuel supply lines, and water supply lines to the heating/cooling system. When that is done he may find himself having to connect electrical wiring to it as well. The technician would then have to run the system and make sure everything goes off smoothly."[15]

The next appointment for the day might be at a new restaurant that needs a refrigeration system, which the HVAC mechanic will install after reading all of the manufacturer's instructions. After determining that all is working well, the mechanic will usually talk to the owner about maintenance of the system and likely sign a contract to service the system regularly, check that it is running correctly, and repair any parts that are causing trouble. These first two appointments would be lengthy jobs, taking the HVAC mechanic all morning.

In the afternoon, a simpler appointment might be on the schedule. All heating and cooling systems need to be regularly maintained, which may involve things like cleaning system components, changing filters, and checking to be sure that nothing is failing or needing replacement. Such a job may take only half an hour, and then the mechanic moves on to the next scheduled appointment—a homeowner who has asked for service because the air-conditioning system is broken. At that job, the HVAC mechanic must diagnose the problem and repair or replace any component that has failed. After testing the system to be sure it is working properly again, the mechanic moves on to the last appointment of the day. Perhaps it is a business that needs a routine checkup of its heating system in preparation for winter. According to Bob, "The efficiency check will identify any impurities the system might have accumulated while in use last season. This will prevent breakdowns when winter comes again as well as save the business money because when the system is running properly, energy costs are lowered."[16]

Bob concludes, "At the end of the day the trained HVAC technician will pack up all his tools: hammers, pipe cutters, torches, voltmeters, pressure gauges, and the like, and head home after a long day of visiting many places and meeting with many people."[17]

Education and Training

Some HVAC mechanics begin their careers with hands-on work experience and apprenticeships, but most take advantage of postsecondary education through trade schools, technical schools, or community college programs leading to an associate's degree. HVAC systems are complex and are constantly being improved and upgraded, so mechanics need a good knowledge base to be successful.

Classroom training for HVAC installers typically lasts between six months and two years. Shorter programs generally lead to an HVAC technician certification, and the longer educational programs provide an associate's degree. About 55 percent of currently employed HVAC mechanics hold a postsecondary certificate, and 16 percent have an associate's degree. Others have a combination of work experience, apprenticeship, and some classroom education. In some states, HVAC mechanics must be licensed in addition to their certification as HVAC technicians or mechanics. In those states, they are required to pass further licensing examinations. Newly certified HVAC mechanics typically are hired to work with experienced technicians for some period of time before performing complicated jobs independently. In addition, HVAC mechanics who work with refrigerants are required to be certified by the US Environmental Protection Agency (EPA) because they handle toxic chemicals.

Many HVAC mechanics also decide to specialize after perhaps one to three years of working as a general technician. Some of these specialties will require advanced HVAC certifications. For example, advanced certifications in HVAC installation are needed in order to supervise installations in the construction of new buildings. Some HVAC mechanics choose to specialize in the installation of oil furnaces or industrial refrigeration operations. Others may become HVAC efficiency analysts or specialize in gas heating. Some go on to be certified as master HVAC mechanics in their specialty areas through further written examinations and practical demonstrations of their skills and abilities.

Skills and Personality

HVAC mechanics need a variety of skills to be successful in their careers. They must have strong math and science skills, especially in physics and chemistry. They need mechanical skills as well, and the ability to pay attention to details and solve problems. When working with clients and customers, HVAC mechanics need interpersonal and communication skills too. They may have to explain intricate technical problems in a way that clients can understand and sometimes must explain why certain repairs or replacements are necessary.

HVAC mechanics also need to be physically fit and have the strength and stamina to lift and move large pieces of equipment. They must be able to work in cramped crawl spaces, in attics, and on rooftops, sometimes for hours at a time. At the same time, they need to have fine motor skills or finger dexterity because they are often manipulating and assembling very small system components.

In general, HVAC mechanics enjoy realistic, practical activities and jobs that demand thinking and investigative skills, determining the facts of a situation, and accomplishing solutions by understanding those facts. HVAC mechanic Greg Mawson specializes in air-conditioning and most enjoys the way that his skills make a real difference for people. He says, "There's nothing that feels better than figuring something out and getting a problem solved. That's the best! You can sit there and brag about it a bit while everybody is reveling in the cool air!"[18]

An HVAC mechanic repairs a faulty air-conditioning unit. People who do this job install, maintain, repair, and clean heating, ventilation, and air-conditioning units in houses and commercial buildings.

Working Conditions

HVAC mechanics work both indoors and outdoors, often in extreme temperatures. During the winter, when they are called to fix heating problems, they are working in cold environments to get them warm again. During the summer, when an air-conditioning system has failed, they may be working in extreme heat until they have solved the problem and gotten the system back online. Some components of heating and cooling systems in large buildings are on rooftops, exposed to all kinds of weather. At other times, the mechanic is working under a house, exposed to water, mud, darkness, and even such creatures as insects or snakes. Working conditions depend on the job and what is required to solve the problem, and an HVAC mechanic does not know what those conditions will be until he or she has arrived at the job site and has determined which part of the system is failing.

Whatever the task, HVAC mechanics have to be safety conscious. According to the US Bureau of Labor Statistics, they have one of the highest risks of injuries and illnesses of all careers. They

Opportunities for Everyone

"While in the past, the HVAC industry was traditionally male-dominated, this image is quickly being shed as more and more women are finding employment in the field. The Bureau of Labor Statistics (BLS Feb. 2017) reported that women make up only 1.4 percent of the HVAC workforce, but the nearly 6,000 women nationwide represents a significant leap from years past. Women's representation is growing in conjunction with the swelling demand for HVAC professionals."

—HVAC Classes, an informational website operated by Sechel Ventures

HVAC Classes, "Ten Scholarships for Women in HVAC," *The HVAC Blog*. www.hvacclasses.org.

may suffer burns, electric shocks, and muscle injuries, and those who work with refrigerants may suffer frostbite or vision damage from the toxic chemicals. HVAC mechanics have to be experts in the dangers of their occupation in order to protect themselves from the risks they face daily.

Employers and Pay

About 64 percent of HVAC mechanics work for plumbing, heating, and air-conditioning contractors or for private HVAC companies. Another 10 percent are in business for themselves. Others may work for large business or retail facilities, local or state governments, private educational institutions, or public health facilities. Median annual pay for HVAC mechanics was $47,080 in 2017.

What Is the Future Outlook for HVAC Mechanics?

Employment numbers for HVAC mechanics are expected to increase by 15 percent through 2026, which is much faster than average for other careers.

Find Out More

ESCO Institute
PO Box 521
Mount Prospect, IL 60056
website: www.escoinst.com

The ESCO Institute is the largest provider in the United States of certification testing and assessment exams for HVAC mechanics and those working with EPA-certified refrigerants. Visitors to the website can view a practice exam in refrigerants, find a list of accredited training programs by state, and discover the areas of certification available to HVAC mechanics.

Explore the Trades
Nexstar Legacy Foundation
101 E. Fifth St., Suite 2100
St. Paul, MN 55101
website: https://explorethetrades.org

This organization is devoted to providing information and inspiration to people interested in careers in the heating, air-conditioning, plumbing, and electrical industries. Its website offers a step-by-step guide to a successful career in these trades.

HVAC Career Now
website: https://hvaccareernow.com

This website lists apprenticeship programs and top schools and colleges for HVAC training. Follow the links to learn more about HVAC and decide whether this career is the right fit for you.

HVAC Classes
website: www.hvacclasses.org

At this extensive website, you can learn in detail what HVAC mechanics do, how they are trained, where to find schools and scholarships, and what different HVAC careers are available.

Wildland Firefighter

What Does a Wildland Firefighter Do?

Wildland firefighters have many different job titles and specialties, but all work in some capacity to control and suppress fires in forest areas and public lands. They work as members of a firefighting crew to put out and contain wildfires, patrol burned areas to find and eliminate hot spots where fires could reignite, create fire lines to deprive fires of fuel, and manage controlled burns to reduce the risk of wildfires under certain conditions. Wildland firefighting crews use water and chemical pumps, high-pressure hoses, heavy equipment and shovels, axes, and power saws to fight fires. They may use specialty equipment, such as all-terrain vehicles and forklifts, aircraft and parachutes, and personal protection safety gear and equipment.

Wildland firefighters may work as part of an engine crew, hand crew, or helitack crew, or they may be hotshots or smokejumpers. Engine crews, usually consisting of between two and ten firefighters, drive the specialized wildland fire engines across rough wilderness roads to fire locations and position the fire engines in safe spots for firefighting. According to the US Forest Service, they "serve as initial attack forces."[19] They fight fires using hand tools and the water or foam on the fire engines.

Other firefighters, such as hand crews and hotshots, fight the wildfire with different skills. Hand crews, which consist of approximately eighteen to twenty team members, typically build fire lines to prevent wildfires from spreading. They use hand tools, power saws, and drip torches and other fire-starting devices, and they are also often responsible for cleaning up burned areas once the wildland fire is out. Hotshots work in twenty-person teams and are like highly specialized hand crews. They suppress and control fires in the most rugged, isolated, and difficult wildland areas.

Other firefighter crews attack the fire from the air. Helitack crews specialize in helicopter operations. Team members may rappel from the helicopter into the fire zone in order to fight the fire with hand tools and chainsaws. They may fly the helicopter to remote locations to drop water or fire retardants from a bucket or tank onto the fire. They also transport other firefighters and equipment to fight fires. Helitack crews may range in size from seven to twenty-four firefighters. Smokejumpers, on the other hand, parachute from airplanes into wildfire areas in teams of eight to twenty, either to quickly suppress an emerging fire or to fight an ongoing fire.

A Typical Workday

No matter what the job, a wildland firefighter does not work a typical eight-hour day. As a matter of fact, he or she does not even work a typical year. Bailey McDade is a wildland firefighter based in Arizona; she works for the US Forest Service. During 2017 she fought fires in Arizona, Oregon, and Montana, logging about two thousand hours during the six summer months of fire season in the western United States. Then she was laid off during the winter. During fire season she sometimes works locally, suppressing small fires, such as at a campground or along the side of a highway. Unlike small fires, major wildland fires require travel and long work assignments. When she and her team-mates are needed for a large fire, they receive a resource order detailing where they are to go and when they should arrive. Mc-Dade says, "We always have a duffel packed with two weeks' worth of clothes and a sleeping bag. We have to be ready for anything."[20]

Once at the site, McDade and her team are responsible for digging fire lines, perhaps a 2-foot-wide (.61 m) swath of bare soil cleared of any material that can burn. Then they set fires on the wildfire side of the fire line to act as buffer zones against the wildfire. As McDade explains, "If you build a mellow enough fire, it won't cross the line; it'll just get sucked into the main wildfire. And once these two fires hit, they extinguish each other because there's nothing left to burn."[21]

After a long day of fighting the wildfire, McDade and the team may return to their fire camp, where tents for sleeping and meals are available. Sometimes, however, they may be working in an area so remote that a real camp is impractical and they simply camp in the woods at a safe distance from the fire. In such cases, she explains, "we usually don't set up tents. We have 10 to 15 minutes from the time we wake up to be completely packed up, geared up, and at our trucks. So most of us, at the end of the day, just lay a sleeping bag down and pass out."[22] Then, in the morning, the day of firefighting starts all over again. Every day, for sixteen or eighteen hours at a time, the team digs fire lines, uses chainsaws to cut down dead trees, and works to suppress the wildfire.

One group of wildland firefighters, smokejumpers, combines skydiving with firefighting. They parachute into wilderness areas so remote that no roads are available. The fires they fight are typically small and have to be suppressed to prevent them from growing and reaching populated areas. Smokejumper Erik Vermaas explains, "We're getting them before they go big. We're catching these fires before they're a problem, before they even get on the news."[23] Smokejumpers may go out in teams of about

A Great Life

"This is the best job ever. What our job description *should* be:

> move dirt
> save forests
> be outside all day
> work hard
> have fun."

—Katie Wimpari, wildland firefighter

Katie Wimpari, "21 Things I Learned as a Woman Wildland Firefighter," *Katalyst Untamed* (blog), December 11, 2017. www.katiewimpari.com.

eight or work independently. Usually, a smokejumper remains in the area for forty-eight hours and fights the fire with chainsaws, shovels, and other hand tools. He or she digs fire lines to surround the fire and cuts down dead trees and brush that would provide fuel for the fire. After the fire seems to be out, the smokejumper has to crawl though the blackened area, feeling charred logs or other suspicious spots for any sparks or smoldering material that could restart the fire. When the job is done, the smokejumper typically hikes out of the area to get to the nearest wilderness road to be picked up by other firefighters. Smokejumpers have physically demanding, highly dangerous jobs, but they love what they do. "The fun part is when you're actually on the front and you're chasing, you're racing the fire," says Vermaas. "That's what we all crave. That's why we're all here."[24]

Education and Training

To become a wildland firefighter, you need a high school diploma and must be between eighteen and thirty-five years old. To be considered for an entry-level position, applicants must pass both a written and a physical exam. The written assessment usually consists of about one hundred questions covering

Firefighting Gear

"We wear long-sleeve yellow button-downs made of a fire-resistant plastic blend that feels like regular cloth. We call them 'yellows'—real fancy. Our cargo pants are the same material; they're dark green and we call them 'greens.' Other than that, we have tall leather boots, leather gloves, a plastic hard hat, and safety glasses. Everybody carries a chainsaw, a Pulaski [ax], a shovel, a hoe, or some other kind of hand tool, plus a big ol' backpack with anything else we might need, including two gallons of water."

—Bailey McDade, wildland firefighter

Quoted in Ashlea Halpern, "Coolest Travel Jobs: What It's Like to Be a Wildland Firefighter," *Afar*, November 28, 2017. www.afar.com.

topics such as spatial skills, logic, and mechanical reasoning. In addition, applicants must pass a difficult physical fitness exam, typically requiring completion of a rugged 3-mile (4.8 km) hike in forty-five minutes while carrying a 50-pound (23 kg) pack.

Once past the initial hiring process, candidates for wildland firefighting complete general fire academy training, which takes about twelve to fourteen weeks. Usually, a rookie is assigned to an engine crew. Then, for those who wish to specialize, such as for helitack crew members or smokejumpers, further aviation training and certifications are required.

Skills and Personality

Wildland firefighters love the outdoors and are dedicated to conserving wilderness areas and protecting people and their homes from fire. They enjoy testing themselves under extreme conditions, are flexible and ready to travel anywhere they are needed, and are excited about facing mental and physical challenges and risks while being of service to others. Wildland firefighters must be able to work closely and communicate clearly with other people—as their lives and the lives of others depend on teamwork. They also must have a tolerance for and ability to deal with stress. In addition, they need to be well coordinated, manually dexterous, and willing to take responsibility to maintain a high degree of physical fitness and stamina.

Working Conditions

Kelly Andersson, a contributing editor for *Wildland Firefighter Magazine*, once described the working conditions of wildland firefighters in a humorous but accurate way:

> Here's one way to find out whether you qualify for work as a wildland firefighter. Stuff what you think you need for a week into a backpack, making sure it weighs at least 50 pounds. . . .
>
> Start hiking cross-country, and make sure you're going at a good clip for at least 10 hours per day on steep slopes — and make sure you're awake for at least 20 hours per day. If you see big movable stuff, such as rocks and logs, pick them up and move them. The bigger they are and the farther and faster you move them, the more it counts. Fall down a lot, and bang yourself up on rocks and roots as often as possible. Thrash around in the brush, get good and scraped, and go without food and water as much as possible. . . .
>
> Get as wet and muddy as possible, and get as hot and dusty and generally filthy as you possibly can. WHATEVER YOU DO, DON'T BATHE.
>
> Keep this up for a week. If you're still alive, and if you think you're having a good time, you may just make it as a wildland firefighter. If you're genuinely having the time of your life and you want more of this, someone may want to hire you.[25]

Employers and Pay

Most jobs for wildland firefighters are through federal agencies such as the Forest Service, the Bureau of Land Management, the Fish and Wildlife Service, and the National Park Service. Others are through state agencies, such as Cal Fire in California or the Colorado State Forest Service. Most positions are located in the western states because that is where wildland fires are most common, but seasonal work is available in almost every state. There are also private companies, generally located in the western United States, that contract out to help on large wildland fires. Landing a wildland firefighter position is a highly competitive process, with many more applicants than there are jobs available, so working with a private company may be a good first step toward the career. In 2018 the average yearly salary for a wildland firefighter was $40,575.

What Is the Future Outlook for Wildland Firefighters?

The job growth for wildland firefighters is expected to be about average, ranging from 5 percent to 9 percent through 2026. Those who are physically fit and experienced are most likely to maintain successful careers.

Find Out More

Colorado Fire Camp
9008 County Road 240
Salida, CO 81201
website: www.coloradofirecamp.com

The Colorado Fire Camp is a training facility for wildland firefighters. Visitors to the group's website can explore the class schedules by semester, learn about being hired as a wildland firefighter, and read reports about historical wildland fires.

National Smokejumper Association
website: http://smokejumpers.com

Dedicated to preserving the history and comradeship of smoke-jumpers and maintaining American forests, this organization offers visitors the opportunity to explore the career and read about the men and women who represent these special wildland firefighters.

National Wildfire Coordinating Group
website: www.nwcg.gov

This federal organization works to coordinate wildfire operations among federal agencies and to establish qualification and performance standards for wildland firefighters. Of particular interest to students is the section "How to Become a Wildland Firefighter" under the "Tool Box" link.

US Forest Service
1400 Independence Ave. SW
Washington, DC 20250
website: www.fs.fed.us

The US Forest Service is a major employer of wildland firefighters. Follow the links on its website under "Managing the Land" or "Science & Technology for Fire" to learn about the different kinds of firefighters and how and why the Forest Service fights fires.

Makeup Artist

A Few Facts

Number of Jobs
5,000 as of 2016

Pay
$22,630 to $124,960 in 2016

Educational Requirements
Makeup artist or cosmetology school and certification

Personal Qualities
A passion for cosmetics; good with people; creative; attentive to detail; self-motivated

Work Settings
Film and video industry; retail department stores; theater and performing arts; fashion shows; salons; bridal boutiques

Future Job Outlook
10 to 14 percent job growth through 2026

What Does a Makeup Artist Do?

Makeup artists are truly artists—they apply cosmetic techniques and processes to the human body, especially the face. They enhance the client's appearance by bringing out the best features and hiding any flaws. At times, makeup artists use their knowledge of the effects of lighting to accomplish this goal, perhaps for a fashion shoot or a wedding album. At other times, perhaps for a modeling show, they know how to create a specific required look, such as enhancing high cheekbones or a certain lip shape. Sometimes makeup artists create an imaginary character, completely changing a face or body, for a movie or for the theater. Whatever the job, these artists know how to apply makeup to achieve the desired look.

There are two main types of makeup artists. Cosmetic or fashion artists work at cosmetic counters in department stores; in the fashion industry; in spas and beauty centers; for private special events, such as parties or weddings; and even for politicians or other public figures who want to present a flawless appearance and emphasize their best features. These makeup artists understand skin types, skin colors, and which colors look best on each individual face. They know how different makeup ingredients affect different faces, and they can use all this knowledge to create beauty.

The second type of makeup artist is the theatrical or film makeup artist. At least half of all makeup artists work in the entertainment industry. These people use their artistic talents to help actors create different characters. The goal of makeup application may vary dramatically, depending on the effect that is desired. Perhaps the makeup artist will make a young actor look older or make an old actor look younger. Perhaps the same actor will be made up to be stunningly beautiful in one scene and flawed and faded in a later scene. Those who are applying makeup for special effects can create the blood and gore needed for horror films, make characters who are supposed to be sick look really sick, or transform an actor into Albert Einstein or Abraham Lincoln. Some makeup artists are adept at creating truly unique science fiction characters.

A Typical Workday

A day in the life of a salon makeup artist may look quite different from the day of an artist working a high fashion show, but they actually have much in common. For both artists, the critical first step of the day is to prepare their makeup kit. The kit consists of a variety of brushes that must be clean and sanitized, a makeup palette consisting of colors for a variety of skin tones, skin-cleansing products, and various other tools and products, such as lip liners, blushes, foundations, and eye shadows. In addition to the makeup kit, a workstation also must be prepared before the first client can be seen.

Dominic Skinner, a London makeup artist, describes a typical day during the annual London Fashion Week. He typically begins early in the morning so as to set up his makeup station backstage and listen to the designer's requirements for the look of

Making It Work

"You have to know how to pick the right makeup for red carpet looks, understand the lighting in different venues, and know how to work well with celebrities. It's something I think I'm really good at. I approach it one client at a time. I always want to be called back, and I want people to like me. I work really hard on building trust, and I never pressure them to book me again. Celebrities don't want to be pressured. They will either like you and ask for you again, or they won't."

—Monika Blunder, celebrity makeup artist

Quoted in Heather Wood Rudulph, "Get That Life: How I Became a Celebrity Makeup Artist," *Cosmopolitan*, May 25, 2015. www.cosmopolitan.com.

each model. Then, he explains, he has perhaps an hour and a half before the show begins to prepare the three models to whom he has been assigned. Skinner says, "Once the models are in line-up, we attack the bodies! We go in with lotion, concealer and foundation to remove any imperfections like bruises, red hands, little cuts, etc. Each model has to look perfect."[26] Then, after the show, he packs up all his tools and makeup and races to the next show of the day. Usually, after doing makeup for two shows, Skinner is finished for the day. But he still has to tidy his makeup kit and wash all the brushes so they will be dry and ready for use the next day.

Makeup artists who work in a salon or freelance with private clients may have similar work schedules, but one major difference is that they consult with each client individually to determine the desired look. Then the artist begins by cleansing the skin, applying primers and foundations, and covering any blemishes with concealers and powders. The final step is applying blush, eyeshadow, and lipstick to achieve the perfect look.

The schedule of a film makeup artist may be quite unlike that of other makeup artists. For one thing, the makeup artist on the set of a movie probably spends all day on the same assignment.

Actors must be made up at the beginning of the day's filming, and alterations and touch-ups are typically required throughout the day. Top film makeup artists create, design, and execute a myriad of special looks. Oscar-winning makeup artist Michele Burke, for example, was responsible for the makeup in the film *Cyrano de Bergerac*. She remembers,

> I had to come up with a design for an iconic character's nose and makeup design on actor Gerard Depardieu. While in the director's . . . office in Paris with Derma wax, I sculpted the nose on the actor, had them approve it then and there. I then took a plaster cast of it, flew back to [Los Angeles], made the noses, and returned to Hungary to shoot it a month later![27]

A makeup artist prepares a fashion model for a show. Makeup artists work in the entertainment and fashion industries and in salons and spas, among other locations.

Burke is accomplished in all areas of makeup, including beauty and fashion, character and period designs, fantasy, and prosthetics (such as sculpting artificial noses). She says, "Being a true and complete makeup artist means being able to do everything."[28]

Father Phantom Studios in the United Kingdom is dedicated to creating special effects for films and special shows. Its cofounders, Ben Fallaize and Laura Viale Durand, create science fiction and fantasy characters using makeup and prosthetics. They cast, sculpt, and mold their creations, first building clay models of the design they want and then painting the creation and adapting the concept to an actor. They not only create faces but also fingers, necks, and other alien body parts. For a completely alien character, makeup application for one actor may take more than four hours to complete.

Education and Training

Although a few makeup artists are self-taught, most obtain formal training, either in cosmetology or aesthetics school. (Currently, there are very few schools offering training specifically as a makeup artist.) In general, cosmetology focuses on hair, skin, and nails, and aesthetics focuses on facial treatments and the application of makeup. Most states require licensing in either cosmetology or aesthetics in order to use the term *makeup artist*, with some requiring aesthetics training and others requiring cosmetology instead. Aesthetics schools typically require between three hundred and eight hundred hours of classroom and practical training, and a cosmetology program requires one thousand to two thousand hours. Once either program is completed, many states require a cosmetologist or aesthetician to pass an exam in order to be certified. Other states have no licensing requirements. People who want to work in film or theater often take further courses in topics such as special effects makeup and prosthetics.

Skills and Personality

Makeup artists love to work with makeup and cosmetics and experiment with different looks. They must be creative and artistic and have an eye for color and detail. In addition, makeup artists need to have excellent people skills. They must be good listeners and communicators, know how to make a client feel comfortable, and have a lot of tact and patience. They also need manual dexterity, stamina to stand and work for long hours, and concentration under pressure. Makeup artists also need to stay up to date on the latest makeup trends and be enthusiastic about their careers.

Working Conditions

Although working conditions vary tremendously depending on specialty areas, almost all makeup artists work under stressful conditions. Sometimes the stress is caused by a demanding, hard-to-please client or by the looming deadline of an event. Other times it is the result of the controlled chaos of a movie studio or a fashion show, both of which require many things to happen at once. Therefore, makeup artists need adaptability and flexibility to cope with different kinds of working conditions.

Makeup artists usually do a lot of traveling and carry their own extensive kits, which they arrange at the makeup station each time they arrive on site. They typically work long, unpredictable hours on the job, and makeup stations may be set up anywhere, from studios to backstage at a theater to vehicles or temporary buildings on location for a film.

Employers and Pay

About one-third of makeup artists are self-employed freelancers. Others work in salons and retail stores, and about half work in the entertainment industry. The lowest-paid makeup artists usually work in stores and salons and are typically paid minimum wage plus tips. Well-known makeup artists in the entertainment industry command top salaries. As of 2016, annual salaries for all makeup artists ranged from $22,630 to $124,960.

What Is the Future Outlook for Makeup Artists?

The employment growth rate for makeup artists is expected to be 10 to 14 percent through 2026. Since the number of people working as makeup artists is relatively small, this means only about six hundred new jobs during that time. The field is highly competitive, but those who stick with it during the first few difficult years are often successful.

Find Out More

Beauty Schools Directory
website: www.beautyschoolsdirectory.com

This website is owned by the Beauty Schools Marketing Group. It offers a detailed description of the makeup artist career and provides a comprehensive list of beauty schools available in the United States and Canada. Search by state and area of interest to find a school that meets your needs.

Chic Studios School of Makeup
Chic Studios NYC
139 Fulton St., Suite 600
New York, NY 10038
website: https://chicstudiosmakeup.com

This national makeup school has locations in New York, Los Angeles, and Denver. It offers school tours for prospective students, and its website details the courses offered and includes a newsletter and blog.

Cosmetology Career Now
website: https://cosmetologycareernow.com

This website, run by a partnership of cosmetology schools, offers information about many areas of cosmetology training, including training to become a makeup artist. Follow the links to find out about schools available, scholarship programs, general information about cosmetology careers, and how to become a makeup artist.

MakeupArtistEdu.org
website: www.makeupartistedu.org

The professionals on this website are dedicated to helping aspiring makeup artists find information about preparing for a career, earning state licensing, starting a business, and more. The site answers questions for those wanting a career in salons, film and television, theater, fashion, and weddings and special events.

Mechanical Engineer

What Does a Mechanical Engineer Do?

According to the mechanical engineering department of Michigan Technological University, "Mechanical engineering is one of the broadest engineering disciplines. Mechanical engineers design, develop, build, and test. They deal with anything that moves, from components to machines to the human body."[29] This means that mechanical engineers apply scientific principles and problem-solving techniques to creating, designing, improving, and manufacturing in such diverse areas as nanotechnology, energy, robotics, and aerospace. Mechanical engineering is all about machines, ranging from the tiniest to the largest. The mechanical engineer uses the science of motion, energy, and force to turn an idea into reality and make anything with moving parts work or work better.

Mechanical engineers can work in many different scientific fields. For example, some concentrate on the field of materials science, focusing on determining the best materials to use with different machines. This kind of mechanical engineering is related to determining the strength, brittleness, and stiffness of materials used in construction, vehicles, and perhaps medical devices so as to design the optimal piece of machinery for a specific use. The field of thermodynamics, on the other hand, focuses on converting energy into useful power, changing one form of energy into another. Mechanical engineers use their knowledge of thermodynamics to design such things as engines, power plants, heating and air-conditioning systems, and refrigerators.

The branches of mechanical engineering are many. Aerospace engineering is one branch and focuses on the design and construction of aircraft. Another branch is thermal engineering, which involves designing heating and cooling systems. Vehicle engineering (both automotive and naval), is a branch that focuses on the design, construction, and operation of the systems that control vehicles. Acoustical engineers represent yet another branch; this one deals with the science of sound. They may help to design a recording studio, develop a better hearing aid, or use an understanding of sound vibrations to design a highway that reduces traffic noise. As a final example, manufacturing engineers focus on the techniques for building quality products that are cost efficient. They design the products and decide how they should be built. They also help to design production plant technologies that make plants run efficiently. This may involve using computer-aided design (CAD) software to help automate the manufacturing process or designing nanomachines. As a matter of fact, in almost all branches of mechanical engineering, computer programs and software are used to design and test new or improved machinery. Mechanical engineers are almost unlimited in the work areas where their analytic, diagnostic, and computer skills may be required.

A Typical Workday

A mechanical engineer's daily schedule is as varied as the branches of mechanical engineering and the specialty areas of each engineer. Despite these differences, most mechanical engineers tend to work with a team, often consisting of others in their field as well as architects, plant managers, and electrical engineers. And most mechanical engineers spend a good amount of time each day in an office setting, working with computer simulations and building prototypes. For example, a typical morning might begin with a team meeting about a problem with the design and functioning of a particular piece of machinery. Together, the team might figure out the best solution to try, and the engineer will spend several hours using a CAD program to design the solution. Then he or she may sit at a workbench and build a small prototype of the piece of machinery, using the computer solution. Finally, the mechanical engineer might test the prototype to see how it might fail; this involves breaking it on purpose, determining how easy it would be to fix, and perhaps even redesigning it.

Problem solving can take up a large part of the mechanical engineer's day, whether the problem is being addressed on a computer or in the real world. Mechanical engineers enjoy both kinds of settings as long as they are resolving mechanical issues. Mechanical engineer Lauren Blas explains, "Some days I am out on a jobsite talking to contractors and figuring out problems in the field, which I really enjoy. But I also love those days when I am trying to solve a design challenge at my desk—bringing out the trace paper and just sketching out ideas."[30]

Mackenzie Lewin works for a company that designs and constructs assembly lines and conveyor belts for car manufacturing companies. She spends a lot of time on a work site to ensure that her designs fit well with the client's needs. She says, "We have to go to the site and take a full assessment of the area so we know all of our restrictions. Like, if there's a column in the middle of the room, we have to know about it so we can design around it. A lot of times, we end up going back and forth to and from the location."[31] Lewin uses a three-dimensional (3-D) imaging technique that uses laser dots to map a room. She takes the information back to her office where she designs CAD models of the machinery and determines their placement in the work area.

Yassmin Abdel-Magied is a well engineer who works for the Shell Oil company in Australia. She travels frequently in her job and works both onshore and offshore. She says there is no typical day and adds,

When I'm onshore, I spend my time helping to prepare for drilling projects, working with geologists to understand what's under ground and then figure out the best rig for each hole.

When I'm offshore working on a rig, I'm supporting the Drilling Supervisor, organising people to get the job done right and designing solutions to make things happen. It's hard work but definitely fun and exciting to see our plans turn into reality.[32]

Education and Training

To become a mechanical engineer, one has to earn a bachelor's degree in mechanical engineering. Many people then pursue a graduate degree in either mechanical engineering or a specialty area. In addition, every state requires a mechanical engineer to

The Best Engine Possible

"I work as a research and test engineer for a major engine manufacturer. Currently, my project entails a lot of engine testing, so I am mostly doing field work in the engine labs. When the data collection is finished, I am the one who analyzes the results and puts them in a nice form using programs like Excel and MATLAB. Occasionally, we have a failure on the engine, and it's my job to determine both why the part failed and what we have to do to ensure it won't fail again. If it happens, it quickly becomes the highest priority and ends up taking up all of my time."

—Dan, mechanical engineer

Quoted in Angela Melick, "Ask an Engineer! What Do Engineers Do Day-to-Day?," *End of Wasted Talent* (blog), March 12, 2010. www.wastedtalent.ca.

obtain a professional engineer's license, which involves passing licensing examinations and gaining some work experience under a licensed engineer.

Skills and Personality

Mechanical engineers are problem solvers; they like to investigate all sides of a problem in order to come up with a solution. Therefore, they must be curious, creative, mathematical, and analytical, and they need advanced computer skills. They also should enjoy a hands-on approach to solving technological issues. At the same time, they are tenacious in the face of challenges. They can immerse themselves in a particular problem and focus single-mindedly until they achieve the desired outcome. In general, mechanical engineers are highly motivated and goal-oriented people.

Mechanical engineers also need to be excellent communicators and team players. Justin is an international mechanical engineer and project engineer working in the construction industry. "Day to day, an engineer in my position spends the vast majority of his time communicating," he explains.

This can be as simple as a conversation with the field personnel talking through possible ways to perform the task to something as complicated as a formal meeting with minutes and presentations and the like. . . . Today, 99% of all engineers work as a member of a team, whether made up of only engineers or a cross-disciplinary team of engineers, specialists and business people.[33]

Working Conditions

Mechanical engineers typically spend a large part of the day in an office setting, but many visit work sites on a regular basis to study and to solve problems with equipment, devices, and work spaces. Their work environments can vary widely. Mechanical engineer Albert Manero works in a clinical research environment. He holds a doctorate in mechanical engineering and is the founder of the nonprofit company Limbitless, which develops prosthetic limbs for children using 3-D printing technology. Manero works in a laboratory, where he leads a team of scientists and engineers. He also conducts clinical trials of his prosthetics and acts as a company spokesman, advocating for medical and financial organizations to support his vision of high-tech prosthetics for children.

Like Manero, Keiren Muir is also a mechanical engineer, but he is employed with Australia's Department of Defense. He works in an office but also aboard naval ships. Muir says, "The best part of my job is how varied the work is. One week I'll be travelling to do testing on a ship somewhere, another week I'll be reviewing engineering design documents."[34]

Employers and Pay

As evidenced by Manero and Muir, mechanical engineers can work in a wide range of industries. These include manufacturing, research and development laboratories, architectural services, automotive industries, aerospace production, biomedical research, robotics, electronic manufacturing industries, energy and power production, and in governmental defense industries. In 2017 the median annual salary for mechanical engineers was $85,880. Those working in research and development had the highest yearly salaries, earning about $98,530. Those in machinery manufacturing earned the lowest at $77,400 per year.

What Is the Future Outlook for Mechanical Engineers?

The mechanical engineering field is predicted to grow by 9 percent through 2026. Job growth rates are expected to be particularly good for those mechanical engineers working in new industries, such as automation, robotics, designing and improving hybrid and electric vehicles, alternative energy, and nanotechnology.

Find Out More

Engineer Girl
website: www.engineergirl.org

This website from the National Academy of Engineering was established to encourage girls and women to consider engineering as a career. Visitors can learn about what engineers do, find interviews with female engineers, and explore many different engineering careers.

EngineeringClicks
website: www.engineeringclicks.com

This website is devoted to providing information for and education about mechanical design engineers. It is an international community and resource where people can read about such topics as 3-D prototypes, CAD systems, thermal designs, and new design materials.

Engineering.com
Toronto West Office
5285 Solar Dr., Suite 101
Mississauga, ON L4W 5B8
Canada
website: www.engineering.com

This organization for engineers and those interested in engineering shares stories from around the world about the latest innovations and challenges in the engineering world. Its website includes fascinating articles about the latest news and research.

Institution of Mechanical Engineers
1 Birdcage Walk
London SW1H 9JJ
United Kingdom
website: www.imeche.org

This international organization promotes mechanical engineering as a career, works to develop engineers and disseminate the latest engineering information, and, in general, works to improve the world through engineering. Visitors to the website can get information about pursuing a career as an engineer.

Farmer

What Does a Farmer Do?

Farmers practice the art and science of agriculture. Agriculture includes the cultivation of land and the raising of plants and crops, as well as the raising of livestock. Farmers raise plants and animals in order to produce products that sustain and enhance life, providing food, fabrics (cotton, leather, or wool, for example) and even wood for building or making paper. They then harvest and sell their products to markets and food companies locally, nationally, and internationally. Farming is as much a lifestyle as it is a career; there are no days off from daily chores and strenuous physical work. There are many different kinds of farmers and an almost unlimited variety of crops and animals that can be farmed, but most farmers specialize in one or just a few agricultural products. Some of the types of farmers are crop farmers, dairy farmers, sheep farmers, cattle farmers, poultry farmers, beekeepers, fish farmers, and vermiculturists (breeders of earthworms to convert waste products into healthy soil).

Many farmers are crop farmers; they plant, grow, and harvest a variety of fruits, vegetables, grains, and forage crops (plants eaten by livestock). Growing plants, however, is far from the only thing crop farmers do. Indiana corn and soybean farmer Brian Bradley explains:

> There's so much more to it than putting a seed in the ground and then picking the produce several months later. There's a huge economics side to it; we're constantly watching the markets trying to get the best price for our product and finding the lowest prices for seed, fertilizer and equipment. Tractors have GPS-guided driving systems now, and many varieties of seeds are bio-engineered. Fertilizers, soil types and weed-killers require an understanding of chemistry. The industry is constantly changing.[35]

Livestock farmers deal with many of these same business issues. They must choose when to market their products, and they need an understanding of science to raise and breed their animals. Livestock farmers raise animals either for meat or for the products they produce, such as milk, eggs, or wool. Whatever the animal or its use, the livestock farmer knows about breeding, diets, medical problems and treatments, and ideal growth rates for the animals. Livestock farmers also need to have mechanical ability because they spend a lot of time using, maintaining, and repairing machinery, whether milking machines or tractors or harvesters.

The majority of modern farmers practice conventional farming, meaning that they take advantage of the chemical and technological advances that enable them to raise the most plants and animals most efficiently and cost effectively. Some farmers, however, specialize in organic farming, either with livestock or crops. Organic crop farmers farm without the use of chemical fertilizers or pesticides. They put a good deal of effort into improving the soil naturally, with substances such as compost, mulch, and manure. Organic livestock farmers raise animals that are never treated with antibiotics and are given feed with no animal by-products and no genetically engineered grains. These animals are given plenty of fresh air and sunshine, whether they are raised for meat or other products.

A Typical Workday

The typical workday for a farmer depends not only on the type of farming but also on the season of the year. Much of the year farmers work long days. Animals have needs that must be met year round. Plants may not need care after harvesting, but fields still have to be maintained. The land may need to be enhanced with winter crops for improving the soil, and farming machinery and farm buildings often require repairs and upkeep. As Bradley explains,

> In the spring most days are spent getting equipment ready for planting. When the weather is right we're in the field planting and drilling seed from sun-up to sundown. After that we go back and spray for weeds, fertilize and spray for weeds again. . . . In late summer, we get equipment ready for harvest. . . . Then, when it's time to harvest, we're in the fields [until] sundown again. The winter tends to be the slowest time, but there's still lots of work hauling the corn and beans to elevators, taking care of the business side of things, getting finances and seed in order for next spring and having a little fun on the snowmobile too.[36]

Jenni and Paul Callahan run a 3-acre (1.2 ha) organic farm in South Carolina. Although the farm is small, their workday, even in winter, is long and full. The Callahans maintain a mixed farm, growing crops and raising animals. They start each morning in the barn, feeding and watering their five dozen chickens and two goats, cleaning the barn and chicken coop, gathering eggs, and milking the goats. Next, they tend to their greenhouse, where they grow crops like kale and lettuce to sell at the local market or from their home. This income, along with the money from selling eggs and handmade goat milk soaps, helps them make it through the winter when income is quite low. During the afternoon, Paul may be planting seeds in trays for the greenhouse while Jenni washes and cartons eggs for sale and harvests and packages greens. Also during the afternoon, regular customers stop by to pick up and pay for orders. By 5 p.m. the goats and chickens are fed again and then brought into the barn and coop for the night since the weather is cold.

During South Carolina's growing season, the Callahans plant and grow vegetables such as tomatoes, peppers, squash, onions, and beets. That is the busy time of year, when they are plowing and planting the land with their tractor and harvesting and selling their crops. Jenni says, "When we have crops in the ground, it is sunup to sundown. We wouldn't do it if we didn't love it, but it is backbreaking work for little pay. This is why there aren't more farmers."[37]

Education and Training

The most important asset a farmer has is experience. Some farmers grew up on family farms and perhaps even inherited their farms. They got their experience over the years of living on a farm. Others are new to farming and need to seek out experience if they are to succeed. One of the most important ways people gain experience is through farm internships. Many small farms offer this experience. Other would-be farmers intern through programs such as the US Department of Agriculture's Beginner Farmer and Rancher Competitive Grants Program. Still others just offer their

A farmer inspects her potato crop to determine when they will be ready to harvest. Some farmers plant, harvest, and sell crops. Others raise livestock. No matter what their specialty, most farmers work long hours.

services as hired help to an established farmer. After three or four years of experience, many feel ready to begin the process of starting their own farms.

Although no formal education is required to become a farmer, most people today do seek relevant education along with experience. They may enroll in college and seek at least an associate's degree in agriculture, agricultural economics, dairy science, farm management, or other areas related to their specific farming interests. Some students acquire bachelor's degrees in agricultural science, farm and ranch management, or perhaps soil science. Others may seek degrees in aquaculture (for fish farming) or horticulture (the science of growing food and ornamental plants). Today's small farms are increasingly specialized in one kind of farming, so it is necessary to acquire the education to make the farm succeed.

Skills and Personality

Farmers must enjoy working outdoors and working with their hands. They need to be good at analyzing issues with land and livestock and operating and maintaining complex machinery. They must have physical strength to complete strenuous tasks, such as lifting heavy objects, repairing fencing, and wrangling large animals. Likewise, they need to be self-motivated, self-disciplined people who can take the initiative each day to maximize the production of their farms.

Many farmers say that it is important to be able to withstand failure and setbacks without being discouraged. Whether a crop fails because of the weather or a flock of chickens is wiped out by disease, farmers have to endure and start over again. According to farmer Forrest Pritchard, "Failure provides us perspective for future enterprises, making us intellectually stronger, more emotionally resilient."[38]

Working Conditions

Approximately 80 percent of the 2.1 million farms in the United States are classified as small farms, while the rest are huge enterprises often referred to as industrial farms or agribusinesses. That means that many farmers work independently, but others manage farming enterprises as employees. Thus, working conditions vary depending on the type of farm.

On all farms, however, farmers are working outdoors, in all kinds of weather, and during all seasons of the year. They are typically performing arduous manual labor, whether it is digging a hole for a fence post or hefting bales of hay to feed cattle or cleaning barns. Crop farmers may spend twelve hours a day driving farm equipment in the fields with only short food and water breaks from the tilling, planting, and harvesting. For some, especially organic farmers, weeding and fighting damaging insects may be a job that has to be done by hand.

Farming is seasonal, meaning that some seasons are busier than others. Seasons that involve planting and harvesting, for instance, are the busiest times for farmers. Even during slower seasons, however, many so-called small farmers have to market

All Worth It

"Often overlooked are the fringe benefits of living on a farm. Things as simple as fresh air, limited noise, few if any 'neighbor' problems and issues to contend with and the freedom of space. Additionally, the simple pleasure of knowing you're feeding other people, growing your own food to the extent you desire, and having a happy dog that has space to run are all aspects that can be forgotten amidst the pressure of harvest and maintenance cycles; but [they] shouldn't be! We make it a point to remind ourselves how lucky we are to live where we do and to be responsible caretakers of land in our local community."

—John Lemondes, a US Army veteran and a new farmer

John Lemondes, "So, You Want to Be a Farmer," Cornell Small Farms Program, Cornell University, Fall 2015. https://smallfarms.cornell.edu.

their own products, plan for planting and breeding, and repair machinery for the next season.

Employers and Pay

Approximately 75 percent of farmers are self-employed. The rest work for large businesses, producing crops, raising livestock, or working in aquaculture. The median income for farmers in 2017 was $69,620.

What Is the Future Outlook for Farmers?

Because large-scale farming is so efficient, many small farms do not make enough profit to survive. As a result, no job growth for farmers is expected through 2026. Nevertheless, opportunities for new farmers do exist. Half of the farmers in the United States today are over fifty-five years old and are close to retirement, so there is room for growth, especially for people interested in spe-cialized markets, such as organic farming. With determination and hard work, new farmers can succeed.

Find Out More

Beginning Farmers

website: www.beginningfarmers.org

This website offers information about many different kinds of farming, how to start a farm, and farm job and internship postings for those who want to gain practical experience on a farm.

The Farmer

website: www.the-farmer.com

Set up specifically for Minnesota farmers, this website offers stories, news, and information of interest to local farmers. Visitors can learn about the issues that matter to typical farmers by reading articles about conservation, weed infestations, government regulations about applying fertilizers, crop rotation, and much more.

Milk Means More

United Dairy Industry of Michigan
2163 Jolly Rd.
Okemos, MI 48864
website: www.milkmeansmore.org

Visit the Milk Means More website, choose the link for "Farming," and learn all about life as a dairy farmer. The website offers an example of a typical day on a dairy farm and features many Michigan farm families, describing how they live their lives and why they love dairy farming.

USDA New Farmers

US Department of Agriculture
1400 Independence Ave. SW
Washington, DC 20250
website: https://newfarmers.usda.gov

The USDA wants to support new farmers and provide the resources to help them get started. On its website, visitors can explore their suitability for farming, learn to make a plan to begin, and find the tools and necessary assistance for becoming farmers.

Surgeon

A Few Facts

Number of Jobs
713,800 in 2016*

Median Pay
$251,890 per year in 2017

Educational Requirements
Medical degree

Personal Qualities
Leadership and decision-making skills; excellent judgment; confident; dedicated to medicine

Work Settings
Physicians' offices; hospitals; academic institutions

Future Job Outlook
14 percent job growth expected through 2026

* includes all physicians (not just surgeons)

What Does a Surgeon Do?

Long ago, during medieval times, physicians left surgical procedures to barbers. Doctors considered themselves intellectuals who did not stoop to manual labor. Today, every physician uses his or her hands to practice clinical medicine, and the surgeon is perhaps the ultimate example of the practical, hands-on approach to helping and healing people. Surgeons treat injuries, diseases, and deformities through operations, cutting into the human body. In the operating room, using a wide variety of instruments and medical devices, the surgeon may, for example, repair bone and tissue injuries; correct a defect, such as a cleft palate or heart defect; remove cancerous tumors; or transplant an organ. As a physician, the surgeon is responsible for preoperative testing and diagnosis of a patient, performing the operation, and providing postoperative care and treatment to ensure a successful patient outcome. He or she is the leader of the medical team and makes the decisions about all aspects of the patient's care.

Many surgeons are considered *general surgeons*, meaning they treat a broad spectrum of diseases and injuries. The American Board of Surgery describes the general surgeon as a specialist in surgery for the digestive system; the abdomen and its contents; breast, skin, and soft tissue; and the endocrine system (glands that produce hormones to regulate body systems). In addition, general surgeons are skilled at critical and emergency care and in treating trauma. General surgeons may diagnose and treat a wide variety of conditions, including removing an inflamed appendix, cutting a cancerous lump from a breast, and removing a bullet from a gunshot wound and repairing the damage. Tim Nelson, a professor of surgery at the University of New Mexico, explains, "We say 'we operate on the skin and all its contents.'"[39]

According to the American College of Surgeons, there are thirteen surgical specialty areas besides general surgery. Some surgeons specialize in neurological surgery. They diagnose and treat conditions of the nervous system, such as the brain and spinal cord, as well as the supporting structures of the nervous system, such as the skull and its blood supply. A neurosurgeon may remove a brain tumor, repair a brain aneurysm (a ballooning blood vessel that can leak or rupture), or surgically close the birth defect for a child born with spina bifida (an open spine). Other surgical specialties include orthopedic surgery (the musculoskeletal system of bones, joints, and muscles), thoracic surgery (conditions within the chest), and ophthalmic surgery (operating on the eye).

A Typical Workday

For surgeons, there is no such thing as a typical day. Each day brings its different schedule of patients, surgeries, and crises and emergencies. What almost all have in common is a fast-paced day with long hours and unexpected events. Joseph A. Ibrahim is a trauma surgeon in the trauma center at Orlando Regional Medical Center in Florida. He starts every day at about 6 a.m. by checking on each patient from the night before to be sure he knows how they are doing. By 7:30 a.m. he is doing morning rounds—visiting and assessing the status of perhaps thirty patients who are hospitalized for a variety of reasons. Some may have traumatic injuries from which they are recovering. Others have had emergency surgery for medical conditions, such as gall bladder removal or appendicitis. On a day when no new emergency situations arise, Ibrahim's schedule may include conferences with his trauma team. "Of course, like a lot of people, my job includes meetings to discuss how our processes are working and how we can improve the protocols," he says. "We also have meetings about individual cases that may be a little more challenging or complex. Plus, because we're a Level 1 Trauma Center, we're required to be a teaching center and are expected to participate actively in research. So we have meetings to discuss the research and the findings."[40]

Peter T. Yu's day is similarly fast paced. He is both a pediatric surgeon (specializing in children) and a thoracic surgeon at the Children's Hospital of Orange County in California. On the hospital's blog, he describes a typical workday. He begins his scheduled time in the operating room by 7:30 a.m. His first patient is a five-year-old boy who needs to have surgery for a hernia, a painful condition that results when tissue bulges out of a weak spot in the abdominal wall. This is a routine surgery for Yu, and it goes well.

At 9 a.m. he and a fellow surgeon operate on a teen boy to repair a chest wall abnormality present from birth. The doctors insert a metal bar between the boy's heart and chest wall to normalize the position of the sternum (breastbone), almost like a dentist uses braces to align teeth in a proper position.

At 10 a.m., Yu makes rounds to check on both postoperative and preoperative patients and discusses their cases with the children's parents and the medical team caring for them. Then, at 10:30 a.m., he prepares for his most complex surgery of the day. It is for a three-month-old infant, and the surgery is known as a thoracoscopic lung lobectomy. It is an operation to repair a rare lung malformation with a mass of abnormal tissue that must be removed. Yu says,

> This is one of my most favorite operations and is my area
> of expertise. . . . Thoracoscopic lung lobectomy is ex-

tremely technically challenging because the surgeon navigates major blood vessels such as the pulmonary artery and pulmonary vein, and operating time can vary from two to six hours depending on a patient's particular anatomy.[41]

Once the operation is successfully completed, Yu's happy job is to tell the parents that the baby is cured and will live a normal life.

Then, during the afternoon, he consults with parents whose children may need surgery for various serious conditions, explains the surgical procedures required and their dangers, and helps them to deal with the plans that must be made. It is a typical day but not an ordinary one. Yu says he always feels blessed to have the meaningful work that he does.

Education and Training

A surgeon's training is extensive and extremely rigorous. After acquiring a bachelor's degree, the prospective physician must complete four years of medical school. The first two years of medical school generally consist of laboratory and classroom work, such as in anatomy, biochemistry, and medical ethics. During the last two years, students begin working with patients, usually in hospitals and clinics and always supervised by licensed physicians.

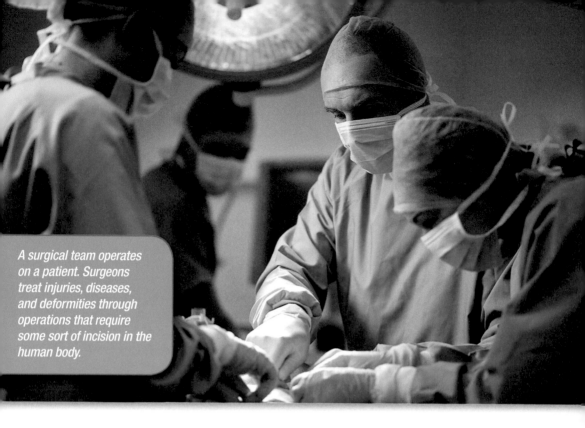

A surgical team operates on a patient. Surgeons treat injuries, diseases, and deformities through operations that require some sort of incision in the human body.

The medical students rotate among different areas of medicine, such as internal medicine, pediatrics, psychiatry, and surgery. It is during this time that medical students decide which areas of medicine most interest them. In the fourth year, students apply for residency programs that match their interests.

Residency programs take between three and ten years to complete, depending on the specialty area. For all new doctors, the first year of residency is called the intern year. For surgical residents, training generally takes about eight or nine years to complete. General surgery residency training is five years. Surgeons who want to specialize further then spend another three years in a fellowship program, perhaps in pediatrics or reconstructive surgery. A surgeon who enters a highly specialized area, such as pediatric heart transplant surgery, may spend ten years after medical school acquiring all the necessary training.

Although surgeons who have completed residencies are considered to be fully trained, they must still obtain a medical license in order to practice medicine. To obtain a license, a surgeon must demonstrate that he or she has graduated from an accredited medical school, completed residency, and passed a national examination. Surgeons who wish to be certified after completing a residency program must pass a specialty certification exam from a certifying board, such as the American Board of Medical Specialties.

Skills and Personality

The American College of Surgeons states that

> first and foremost, surgeons are trained, not born. Facility with knot-tying and sewing is handy, but some of the most wise and revered surgeons in practice today were not known for their dexterity when they were medical students or junior surgery residents. Intelligence, professionalism, conscientiousness, creativity, courage, and perseverance on behalf of your patients are the critical factors.[42]

Surgeons have to have good judgment, be adept at leadership and quick decision making, have confidence in themselves, and be highly motivated to make a difference in their patients' lives. They also must be patient, compassionate, and good at communicating with people. Manual dexterity, physical stamina to endure long hours in the operating room, and strong attention to detail are required as well.

Working Conditions

Surgeons work in physicians' offices, clinics, and hospitals. Some also work in academic institutions, research facilities, and for the federal government. In hospital operating rooms, they work under sterile conditions and lead medical teams, which include other doctors, nurses, and supporting staff. Surgeons typically work long, irregular hours, often standing for long periods of time while bent over a patient. They average between fifty and sixty hours a week and can be on call for emergency situations or phone consultations at any time of the day or night.

The Trials of Residency for a Surgeon

"I loved being fully immersed in surgery. Understanding the nature of the ways in which the human body can be altered by infection, inflammation, tumors and trauma is completely engrossing. Being able to reverse those processes in a single day is even more so. It can be all-consuming. And for many surgeons, it is the pursuit of these experiences that gives meaning to their lives. However, the time away from my family was painful. . . . I rarely saw my children during the last years of residency. I spent far more hours with my patients and my colleagues than I spent with my husband and kids."

—Niamey Wilson, breast cancer surgeon

Niamey Wilson, "The Secret World of Women Surgeons You Had No Idea Existed," *Huffington Post*, December 6, 2017. www.huffingtonpost.com.

Employers and Pay

Surgeons work in group practices, health care organizations, and hospitals. Their average annual income as of 2017 was $251,890.

What Is the Future Outlook for Surgeons?

The demand for surgeons continues to increase. The job growth rate for surgeons is expected to be faster than average at about 14 percent through 2026.

Find Out More

American College of Surgeons

633 N. Saint Clair St.
Chicago, IL 60611
website: www.facs.org

This organization's website offers educational resources for students interested in becoming surgeons. Of particular interest is the section titled "So You Want to Be a Surgeon," which discusses the kind of advice and information that medical students need when they are deciding on a surgical career. It includes a long section describing all fourteen surgical specialties.

American Medical Association (AMA)

330 N. Wabash Ave., Suite 39300
Chicago, IL 60611
website: www.ama-assn.org

The AMA is an organization of physicians dedicated to promoting the science of medicine and improving public health. To learn about their efforts in the area of medical training and the latest news about the issues facing medical students and residents, follow the "Education" link on its website.

Association of American Physicians and Surgeons

1601 N. Tucson Blvd., #9
Tucson, AZ 85716
website: https://aapsonline.org

This nonprofit organization is devoted to preserving the doctor-patient relationship. Visitors to the website can access informative articles about issues such as medical ethics, Medicare, disaster preparedness, economics, and politics related to medical care.

Royal College of Surgeons

35-43 Lincoln's Inn Fields
London WC2A 3PE
United Kingdom
website: www.rcseng.ac.uk

This British professional organization of surgeons maintains an extensive website that provides detailed information for those interested in a surgical career. Sections include topics for students, women in surgery, residencies, and more.

Source Notes

Hands On

1. Careers and Employability Service, "Choosing a Career: Finding the Right Career for You," University of Kent. www.kent .ac.uk.
2. Thomas Zacharias, "Why I Became a Chef," *Livemint* (blog), October 16, 2015. www.livemint.com.
3. Fieldlens Team, "7 Reasons Why It's Great to Work in Construction," *Industry News* (blog), Fieldlens. https://fieldlens .com.

Electrician

4. Quoted in *Power Partner MN Blog*, "A Day in the Life of an Electrician," November 22, 2017. https://powerpartnermn .com/blog.
5. Quoted in Jeremy Anderberg, "So You Want My Trade: Electrician," *Art of Manliness* (blog), September 24, 2015. www .artofmanliness.com.
6. Quoted in Tonia Nifong, "A Day in the Life of an Electrician: Michael Lucas," *Electrical Blog*, Berwick Electric Company, October 16, 2013. www.berwickelectric.com.
7. Quoted in Nifong, "A Day in the Life of an Electrician."
8. Independent Electrical Contractors, "Apprenticeship: Careers." www.ieci.org.

Plumber

9. Quoted in Candace Roulo, "A Career in Plumbing Can Lead to Many Paths," *Candace Roulo Blog*, *Contractor*, July 24, 2012. www.contractormag.com.

10. Quoted in Ann Carrns, "For Plumbers, It's All About the Sweet Smell of Money," *Marketplace*, March 25, 2014. www.market place.org.
11. Quoted in Jeremy Anderberg, "So You Want My Trade: Plumber," *Art of Manliness* (blog), October 18, 2018. www .artofmanliness.com.
12. Quoted in Anderberg, "So You Want My Trade: Plumber."
13. Quoted in Kelly Faloon, "Women in Plumbing: A Rewarding Career," *Plumbing & Mechanical*, July 20, 2016. www.pm mag.com.

HVAC Mechanic

14. Dan Robbins, "What You Should Know About Starting an HVAC Career," ToughNickel, April 15, 2018. https://tough nickel.com.
15. Bob, "An Average Day for an HVAC Technician," HVAC Training 101. https://hvactraining101.com.
16. Bob, "An Average Day for an HVAC Technician."
17. Bob, "An Average Day for an HVAC Technician."
18. Quoted in Zander Buel, "Graduate Connections—Meet Greg Mawson," *Refrigeration School Blog*, October 2, 2018. www .refrigerationschool.com.

Wildland Firefighter

19. US Forest Service, "Engine Crews." www.fs.fed.us.
20. Quoted in Ashlea Halpern, "Coolest Travel Jobs: What It's Like to Be a Wildland Firefighter," *Afar*, November 28, 2017. www.afar.com.
21. Quoted in Halpern, "Coolest Travel Jobs."
22. Quoted in Halpern, "Coolest Travel Jobs."
23. Quoted in Rachel Monroe, "Superheroes Are Real," *B/R Mag*, Bleacher Report, October 11, 2016. https://thelab.bleacher report.com.
24. Quoted in Monroe, "Superheroes are Real."

25. Kelly Andersson, "So You Want to Be a Firefighter?," *Wildland Firefighter Magazine*, April 1997. www.wildfirenews.com.

Makeup Artist

26. Quoted in *Irish News*, "A Day in the Life of a Professional Makeup Artist During London Fashion Week," February 17, 2017. www.irishnews.com.
27. Quoted in *Makeup Armoury Blog*, "On Set with . . . Michele Burke," August 22, 2017. www.themakeuparmoury.com.
28. Quoted in *Makeup Armoury Blog*, "On Set with . . . Michele Burke."

Mechanical Engineer

29. Michigan Technological University, "What Is Mechanical Engineering?," 2018. www.mtu.edu.
30. Quoted in CannonDesign, "A Day in the Life of a Mechanical Engineer," *Consulting-Specifying Engineer*, December 30, 2016. www.csemag.com.
31. Quoted in Josh S. Rose, "The Mechanical Engineer: What It's Like for Mackenzie Lewin to Work in a Field Dominated by Older Men," *America at Work*, Medium, August 3, 2018. https://medium.com.
32. Quoted in Institution of Mechanical Engineers, "Yassmin Abdel-Magied, AMIMechE, Well Engineer, Shell." www.im eche.org.
33. Quoted in Angela Melick, "Ask an Engineer! What Do Engineers Do Day-to-Day?," *End of Wasted Talent* (blog), March 12, 2010. www.wastedtalent.ca.
34. Quoted in Josephine Parsons, "What It's Really Like to Work as a Mechanical Engineer," Junkee, July 25, 2018. https://junkee.com.

Farmer

35. Quoted in Brett McKay, "So You Want My Job: Farmer," *Art of Manliness* (blog), November 2, 2018. www.artofman liness.com.
36. Quoted in McKay, "So You Want My Job."
37. Quoted in Jenn Morson, "So You Want to Flee the City and Become a Farmer," CityLab, January 23, 2017. www.citylab .com.
38. Forrest Pritchard, "9 Rules for Starting Your Own Farm," *Art of Manliness* (blog), November 27, 2017. www.artofman liness.com.

Surgeon

39. Quoted in Nancy LeBrun, "9 Things Your General Surgeon Wants You to Know," HealthGrades, November 18, 2018. www.healthgrades.com.
40. Joseph A. Ibrahim, "A Day in the Life of a Trauma Surgeon," *Orlando Health Blog*, March 14, 2018. www.orlandohealth .com.
41. Peter T. Yu, "A Day in the Life of Pediatric Surgeon Dr. Peter Yu," *CHOC Children's* (blog), April 17, 2017. https://blog .chocchildrens.org.
42. American College of Surgeons, "Section I: Surgical Traits." www.facs.org.

Interview with an HVAC Mechanic

Ronnie Long is a master HVAC mechanic who has been operating his own business in Kenbridge, Virginia, for thirty-two years. He specializes in the installation, maintenance, and repair of oil furnaces and heat pumps. He answered questions in an in-person interview with the author.

Q: Why did you become an HVAC mechanic?

A: I was out in the tobacco field at the end of August; it was 105 degrees, and we were topping and suckering tobacco. And my uncle drove up and started talking to me and asked me what I was planning on doing the rest of my life. I told him I wasn't sure. I hadn't really decided yet. And he said, "You ought to go down to the college and take up plumbing, and you could make more money than a doctor." As the day in the field progressed, it got to sounding better and better. So the next morning I called the college and set up an appointment with the admissions counselor. After lunch, I went down to talk to her, and she recommended taking up air-conditioning, heating and refrigeration, and electricity. (They didn't have plumbing classes.) So I signed up to take those classes. I took three years' worth of classes in two years and graduated. Once I graduated, I started my own little business out of a Ford Ranger truck with a camper shell on the back.

Q: Can you describe your typical workday?

I begin my morning with breakfast and the news while I wait for phone calls to come in. I then spend most of the morning getting everything lined up and organized for the jobs for the day. Often I have to pick up materials to complete my service calls. I also take this time to look at and bid on my jobs. I then start with emergency calls first, and once they are completed, I start my regular service calls for the day. And then once I get my service calls completed,

I go do my installation jobs. I do those in the evenings. My typical day is going to be twelve hours, but if I want to arrange some time off, like to go to my son's ballgame or something, I can do that.

Q: What do you like most about your job?

A: I like the most being able to please the customers, communication with the customers, and being able to have the customers happy—earning their trust. I really like building relationships with the customers.

Q: What do you like least about your job?

A: After a long day, sitting down and trying to take care of the paperwork part of my business is very difficult. Paperwork would include invoices, figuring bids for jobs, writing material lists for ordering parts, and organizing for taxes. I'd rather be out working with my hands and accomplishing something. Thirty minutes of paperwork is more tiring to me than four hours of labor.

Q: What personal qualities do you find most valuable for this type of work?

A: You need to be very patient and people oriented. You need to be able to communicate with people and get along with people of all different personalities. You need to be honest so that you can build up your relationships. And everything else hinges around that.

Q: What advice do you have for students who might be interested in this career?

A: If you are a motivated person that wants to be able to work anywhere in any part of the country and have a job that you're not easily replaceable in (which makes you very valuable), a trade is a quick way to start a career without having to invest years and years in college. You can start small with very little up-front costs and build your business as you go. Also, you would be able to be hired by companies that are looking for tradesmen. Tradesmen are in great demand and in high-paying positions too. If you've got a trade, you can get a job right away.

Other Careers If You Like Working with Your Hands

Aircraft service technician
Architect
Athletic trainer
Automotive mechanic
Bartender
Blacksmith
Broadcast technician
Carpenter
Casino dealer
Computer technician
Construction manager
Dental hygienist
Environmental engineering
  technician
Forensic science
  technician
Graphic designer
Hairstylist

Nuclear equipment operator
Nurse
Occupational therapist
Paramedic
Pet groomer
Physical therapist
Pipe fitter and steam fitter
Radio mechanic
Sign language interpreter
Skincare specialist
Solar photovoltaic installer
Structural iron and steel
  worker
Surveyor
Truck driver
Veterinarian
Veterinary technician
Welder

Editor's note: The online *Occupational Outlook Handbook* of the US Department of Labor's Bureau of Labor Statistics is an excellent source of information on jobs in hundreds of career fields, including many of those listed here. The *Occupational Outlook Handbook* may be accessed online at www.bls.gov/ooh.

Index

Picture Credits

About the Author

Toney Allman holds degrees from Ohio State University and the University of Hawaii. She currently lives in Virginia, where she enjoys a rural lifestyle as well as researching and writing about a variety of topics for students.